THE HUNDRED YEARS WAR

A History from Beginning to End

Copyright © 2019 by Hourly History.

All rights reserved.

Table of Contents

Introduction
Background
The War Begins: 1337-1360
First Peace: 1360-1369
The Caroline War: 1369-1389
Second Peace: 1389-1415
England Triumphant: 1415-1429
French Revival: 1429-1453
Peace at Last
Legacy
Conclusion

Introduction

Wars, by their very nature, tend to be relatively short. They use resources, consume manpower, and weaken the nations involved. Most countries simply cannot sustain wars for extended periods. World War I lasted for four years, World War II lasted for six, and both conflicts had devastating consequences for all the combatant nations. But, during what has become known as the Age of Chivalry, one series of conflicts between two of the most powerful nations in Europe continued through five generations of kings and for more than one hundred years.

What has become known as the Hundred Years' War was a conflict between the House of Plantagenet, the ruling dynasty in England, and the House of Valois, rulers of the kingdom of France. The war began in 1337 and did not finally end until 1453. This was the most notable and protracted war of the Middle Ages, and it contributed directly to the creation and emergence of the national identities of modern England and France.

Both countries poured money and men into the war which ebbed and flowed with first one side gaining the advantage and then the other. At one point England, following stunning military victories at Crécy and Agincourt, controlled much of present-day France. Later, French victories at Orléans and Castillon turned the tide in favor of the House of Valois. When the war began, national armies were made up of mercenaries and peasants conscripted by their feudal lords. By the time that it ended, the first standing armies of the modern era had been created and were composed mainly of professionals who specialized in conflict. The final major engagement of this war was also the first European battle to be decided partly by gunfire.

The Hundred Years' War shaped the history of modern Europe and changed the very nature of warfare. It was also one of the longest and most significant conflicts ever to have been fought in mainland Europe. This is the story of the Hundred Years' War.

Chapter One

Background

*"A Knight ther was, and that a worthy man,
That from the tyme that he ferst bigan
To ryden out, he lovèd chyvalrye,
Trouth and honoúr, fredóm and curtesie."*

—Geoffrey Chaucer, The Canterbury Tales

The origins of the disputes that led to the Hundred Years' War can be traced back to 1066 when William the Conqueror, duke of Normandy, invaded England and established himself as king of the country. In addition to ruling England, William also retained control of Normandy, the northwestern part of present-day France. Normandy at that time was a virtually independent principality that owed only limited allegiance to the kingdom of France which controlled the territory to the south of the Middle Seine.

William's kingdom therefore comprised England, parts of Wales, and a swathe of northwestern France. Subsequent English kings increased the territory in France which they controlled. Henry II, who ruled from 1154 to 1189, added the duchy of Brittany, Aquitaine, and Anjou, all in the western part of present-day France, to the lands controlled by the English. The main branch of the royal house of England, the Plantagenets, became known as the Angevins (from Anjou). During the next 150 years, there were frequent armed confrontations between the kingdom of France and England over the right to rule these western territories.

King John, who ruled England from 1199 to 1216, suffered a series of disastrous losses which saw France regain control over Normandy and Anjou and a French army landed in England with the aim of taking control of the country for Prince Louis of France. This invasion was repulsed, and John's son, Henry III, was able to salvage control over Aquitaine under the Treaty of Paris which was signed in 1259 and brought the conflict between France and England to a temporary end.

In the early years of the fourteenth century, the English king was Edward II, crowned in 1307. Edward found himself embroiled in a war with Robert the Bruce, the king of Scotland and himself a descendant of Norman nobility. Robert was attempting to re-conquer parts of Scotland taken by earlier English kings and to establish Scotland as an independent kingdom. The war against Scotland went badly for Edward, and in 1324, the Pope formally recognized Robert as the king of an independent Scotland. The Scottish king lost little time in signing an alliance with the kingdom of France, and suddenly, England found itself between a potentially hostile France to the south and an independent Scotland to the north.

In 1327, Edward II was deposed in favor of his son, Edward III, with the assistance of the French king. Edward III was just 14 years old when he took the throne, but he quickly proved to be an altogether more effective and capable ruler than his father. He renounced all claims to the throne of Scotland in 1328 and concluded an alliance with the Scots, largely nullifying the threat from the north. This was important to England because tensions with France were increasing, and with the Franco-Scottish alliance, there was a real risk of England facing a war on two fronts. Although there were further sporadic conflicts between the Scots and the English, the treaty agreed in 1328 made the prospect of France and Scotland waging a combined war against England less likely.

During the early 1330s, France launched a number of seaborne attacks on English ports. Most were small-scale harassing attacks, but many people in England feared a full-scale French invasion. The situation was further complicated by the intermarriage between members of the ruling houses in Europe. When the king of France, Charles IV, died in 1328, the question of his successor was extremely complex. Charles left no direct male heir and Edward III, the king of England, was Charles's nephew through his mother, Isabella of France, and therefore Charles's closest male relative. Perhaps unsurprisingly, the French rejected the notion of a ruler who would make England and France into a single kingdom and instead the French throne was passed to a first cousin of Charles IV who became King Philip VI of France in 1328. Philip was also the first member of the House of Valois to rule France.

Although it was clear that Edward III resented the new French king and felt that he had a better claim to the French throne, he seemed to accept the decision of the French jurors who had elected Philip. However, Edward III was also the duke of Aquitaine, the last remaining English territory in France, and in this role, he was required to pay homage to the king of France. Still resentful of the rejection of his claim to the French throne, Edward refused to do this as required in 1337. Philip responded by immediately confiscating all English lands and holdings in Aquitaine. This event is usually taken to mark the beginning of the Hundred Years' War, but it did not in fact lead to immediate conflict between England and France. However, the confiscation of lands in Aquitaine did prompt Edward to renew his claim on the French throne and in early 1340 to declare himself king of France and the French Royal Arms.

Edward's claim to the French crown was recognized by a number of cities in the Low Countries, and the half-brother of the count of Flanders paid homage to Edward as king of France. On June 22, 1340, Edward left England with a fleet of 150 small merchant ships known as cogs, which had been converted for use as warships, headed for the Zwin estuary off the Flemish coast. Their final destination was the port city of Sluys in Flanders. Between the English fleet and the Flemish coast, however, was a fleet of 213 French, Castilian, and Genoese warships under the command of French admiral and noble Hugues Quiéret.

On June 24, 1340, the two fleets engaged in battle in the opening engagement of what would become the Hundred Years' War.

Chapter Two

The War Begins: 1337-1360

"Evil to him who evil thinks."

—Edward III of England

The naval engagement which became known as the Battle of Sluys involved very different tactics on each side. The French fleet arranged their fleet in three lines, using ropes and chains to join their ships together to create three large fighting platforms filled with crossbowmen and men-at-arms. However, after a day of almost continual wind and rain, by mid-afternoon the lines of the French fleet had become entangled and, even worse, they were downwind of the English fleet. Edward saw his opportunity and sent his smaller fleet into the fray.

English tactics were novel—they used small formations of three ships, two filled with archers flanking one carrying men-at-arms, and each group of three English ships would attack a single French vessel. It soon became apparent that the longbows used by the English archers were superior to the crossbows used by the French as they had longer range and were capable of a much higher rate of fire. During the evening and into the night, the English ships continued to pick off the French warships one by one until finally, the last remnants of the French fleet attempted to escape. Only

17 French warships managed to break out; the remainder were destroyed or captured.

French casualties were around 16,000 to 20,000 killed, including their admiral. The English lost four knights and a handful of fighting men. It was, as one modern historian has pointed out, "a naval catastrophe on a scale unequalled until modern times." The immediate effect of the battle was to remove the threat of a French invasion of England. The French navy was much larger than the English and the losses were quickly replaced, but English ships retained control of the English Channel for the remainder of this first phase of the war. This victory also allowed Edward to land his army and to begin the land war by laying siege to the city of Tournai in Flanders.

Sieges were a common means of making war in this period and were to characterize most of the Hundred Years' War. Pitched battles between large armies were relatively rare, and it was far more common for both sides to use siege tactics to gain control of enemy cities. Armies in this period, often called the Age of Chivalry, comprised relatively small numbers of nobles, usually mounted, wearing heavy plate armor and carrying a variety of weapons. These knights were bound by a complex code of conduct and obeyed three masters: their feudal lord or king, their lady, and God. Knights were supplemented by large numbers of less well-armored freemen, wearing chain mail and often using weapons such as pikes, and by large numbers of mercenaries.

Projectile weapons were provided by crossbowmen in most armies and longbowmen in the English armies. Longbowmen were highly trained and could unleash anything up to 12 shots per minute. Longbows had great range (up to 300 feet) and were capable of piercing mail armor. Against these bows, crossbows were limited to a lesser rate of fire and range but were capable of piercing both plate and chain armor.

Sieges rarely led to a quick result, and the siege of Tournai dragged on until September 1340 without the city being taken. By that time Philip VI had arrived in the area with his army, though he was reluctant to meet the English in battle. By September 25, both the French and English kings were running short of money and neither could afford to continue fighting. A truce was arranged, known as the Truce of Espléchin, causing the English to withdraw.

The peace lasted for just nine months until a new dispute about succession led to another round of military engagements between the French and the English. The issue on this occasion was the duchy of Brittany in northwestern France. In April 1341, the duke of Brittany died with no male heirs. His closest living relative was his half-brother John, sixth earl of Richmond. Traditionally, it was the responsibility of the French king to decide on disputed succession in Brittany or any other French province, but John was not confident that Philip would recognize his right since he had close connections to England and Philip's nephew also coveted the duchy. Instead, John declared himself to be count of Montfort, raised an army, and by August, he was in control of the three main Breton cities, Nantes, Rennes, and Vannes.

Philip, who supported the rival claimant to the duchy, his nephew Charles of Blois, sent a French army to Brittany. All the main cities in the region were quickly recaptured, and John of Montfort was arrested and taken to Paris. Although the Truce of Espléchin was still in force, Edward sent an English army to Brittany, and by January 1343, the English had taken Vannes and were besieging Rennes. The French army was approaching, and a major battle looked likely when two cardinals dispatched by the Pope arrived and forced Edward and Philip to agree on another truce, the Truce of Malestroit.

This lasted until mid-1346 when Edward arrived on the Cotentin Peninsula of Normandy with an army of 10,000 men. For more than a month, the English army moved through Normandy, besieging and capturing several major cities including Caen. Then, in August 1346, the English and French armies finally met in battle near the town of Crécy-en-Ponthieu. The French army was much larger— historians suggest that it comprised something between 20,000 and 30,000 men. Opposing them was a much smaller English army of 7,000 to 15,000. Still, just as in the Battle of Sluys, the English longbows proved to be much more effective than the French crossbows.

The battle was another catastrophic defeat for the French. It has been estimated that as many as half of the French forces may have died at Crécy. There is some doubt about English losses, but these are believed to have been less than 1,000. The French army was crippled and humiliated by this massive defeat and was, in the short term, unable to oppose the advance of the English army in Normandy.

In 1347, Edward's army captured the vital port city of Calais and looked set for other important gains when a new factor entered the war: the Black Death. This plague was one of the most devastating pandemics ever and led to the deaths of an estimated 75 to 200 million people. England and France were both affected, and this meant that Edward was unable to reinforce his army or to finance the hire of new troops. The conflict in Normandy descended into a stalemate with neither side being strong enough to directly challenge or defeat the other.

In 1350, Philip VI died and his son, John II, became the new king of France. However, it wasn't until the mid-1350s that the effects of the Black Death had receded sufficiently for both sides to resume the war. Edward III's son, Edward the Black Prince, launched a major invasion of French territory. In September 1356, the Black Prince was met by a much larger French army near the town of Poitiers. Once again, the English archers proved formidable; the French army was defeated and their king captured. John II would spend nearly all of the remainder of his reign as a prisoner in London.

Negotiations followed as the English set the ransom required for the release of the French king. The French were unable to raise the four million écus demanded, and John remained a prisoner. Discontent in France led to a peasant revolt in 1358 which left many castles destroyed and nobles killed. Capitalizing on French weakness, Edward sent another army to France in the summer of 1359. The English army besieged Rheims and even attacked Paris before a freak event persuaded Edward that God disapproved of this venture. While it was garrisoned in the city of Chartres, the English army was afflicted by a hailstorm of titanic proportions at Easter 1360. More than 1,000 English soldiers and 6,000 horses were killed in the deluge, which became known as Black Monday, and Edward vowed to God to make peace with France.

When the French dauphin, Charles (who would later become King Charles V) who ruled France in the absence of John, offered negotiations, Edward was happy to agree. In October 1360, the two sides agreed to the Treaty of Brétigny. This brought the conflict to an end. Edward agreed to renounce his claim on the French throne and in exchange, England was given control over the city of Calais and the region of Aquitaine. With the signing of this treaty, the first phase of the Hundred Years' War, often called the Edwardian War, came to an end.

Chapter Three

First Peace: 1360-1369

"War is the greatest plague that can afflict humanity, it destroys religion, it destroys states, it destroys families. Any scourge is preferable to it."

—Martin Luther

In 1364, John II died in captivity in England. He was succeeded by his son, who became King Charles V. Even before Charles took the throne, he faced a threat to his kingdom from within. The kingdom of Navarre in the Basque region close to the Pyrenees in Gascony took advantage of the absence of the king in 1363 to mount a rebellion against the French crown. Although France and England were technically at peace, Edward covertly supported the Charles II of Navarre and hoped that this revolt would further weaken the French. However, just three days before his coronation, Charles V and his armies utterly defeated the forces of Navarre at the Battle of Cocherel.

Although there was no direct military confrontation between France and England during the brief peace, there was no lack of fighting in western Europe. One of the main points of conflict was a dispute over the succession to the throne of the kingdom of Castile, part of present-day Spain. In 1366, the kingdom was ruled by Peter of Castile. His half-brother Henry of Trastámara disputed Peter's right to the throne and raised an army to take control of the region. Edward the Black Prince of England supported Peter while Charles V of France supported Henry. The French supplied 12,000 troops to assist Henry in a successful invasion of Castile and Peter was forced into exile in English-controlled Aquitaine.

The Black Prince was at this time the ruler of Aquitaine, and he decided to support Peter by raising an army against Henry. He did this in the name of Aquitaine rather than England to avoid breaking the terms of the Treaty of Brétigny. The army led by the Black Prince and Peter defeated the forces of France and Henry at the Battle of Nájera in April 1367, and Peter was restored to the throne of Castile.

Although the campaign to restore Peter as the ruler of Castile was successful, it was also ruinously expensive. The Castilians had agreed to recompense the Black Prince for his expenditure during the war, but in the event, they were not able to do this. When he returned to Aquitaine with his army, the prince was unable to pay his men, and many formed groups of brigands who roamed the countryside looting and stealing both in Aquitaine and neighboring Gascony. This lawlessness infuriated the French lords of Gascony and the French king.

In desperate need of money, the Black Prince called an assembly of the Parliament of Aquitaine in early 1368 and persuaded them to allow him to raise a *fouage*, or hearth tax, of ten sous for the next five years. This was a tax which was to be levied on virtually every household in English-controlled Aquitaine, and it was extremely unpopular. Several of the French lords of Aquitaine used the imposition of the tax as a reason to rebel against English rule. One of the most influential, Arnaud-Amanieu VIII, lord of Albret, who had fought alongside the Black Prince in Castile, petitioned Charles V for his support in a rebellion against English rule. The French king summoned the Black Prince to Paris to have a case heard there in the high court. The prince, angered by this, replied that "We will willingly attend at Paris on the day appointed since the king of France sends for us, out it shall be with our helmet on our head and sixty thousand men in our company."

The Black Prince also imprisoned the French king's messengers, a deadly insult. In response, some French lords of Aquitaine revolted and attacked the English high-steward of the city of Rouergue, killing a number of his men. The rebellion against English rule spread throughout Aquitaine, and by the beginning of 1369, more than 900 castles and towns throughout the region were in open revolt. The Black Prince himself was extremely ill by this time and unable to personally lead military operations.

In spring of 1369, Charles V of France formally declared war on England because of the rebellion in Aquitaine. In response, Edward III once again declared himself to be the rightful king of France. Charles responded by announcing that all English possessions in France were forfeit. Thus, England and France once again found themselves at war in what became known as the Caroline War, the second phase of the Hundred Years' War.

Chapter Four

The Caroline War: 1369-1389

"This royal throne of kings, this scepter'd isle,
This earth of majesty, this seat of Mars,
This other Eden, demi-paradise."

—John of Gaunt, Act 2 Scene 1, *Richard II* by William Shakespeare.

When the war resumed, England lacked competent military leaders. Edward III was 57 years old, an advanced age for the time, and he was no longer able to lead his forces in battle. His son, Edward the Black Prince, was so ill with what is thought to have been dysentery that he was unable even to mount a horse. This left Sir John Chandos, the seneschal of Poitou and one of the Black Prince's closest friends, as the main English tactician. Chandos had been involved in the English victories at the battles of Crécy and Poitiers, and he was widely regarded as a very able leader.

When the French army began its advance in 1369 and took the towns of La Roche-Posay and Saint-Savin, Chandos led a night attack intended to reclaim the important abbey of Saint-Savin. This wasn't a battle, it was a minor skirmish, but Chandos was killed leaving the English without an experienced military leader. In the spring of 1370, the French armies moved into Aquitaine, and many towns formerly under English control were retaken including the city of Limoges which surrendered on the orders of its bishop. The Black Prince swore that he would recapture the city, and in September 1370, he set out with an army of around 4,000 men. By this time, he was so weak that he was unable to mount his horse and he had to be carried into battle in a litter.

Limoges was retaken by the English, and the city was pillaged and many of its inhabitants massacred as a punishment for its surrender. The Black Prince had intended to execute the bishop who had surrendered the town, but he was dissuaded from this by his followers. Following the fighting at Limoges, the Black Prince returned to Cognac. He would never again be strong enough to lead an army in battle, and soon after, he returned to England, extremely ill and virtually destitute.

Meanwhile, the French advance into Aquitaine continued. Charles V deliberately avoided open battle with the English and instead pursued a policy of the gradual re-acquisition of towns in the region by siege. This was a slow process, but it meant that larger and larger areas of formerly English Aquitaine fell under French control. The city of Poitiers fell in 1372, and Bergerac followed in 1377. The English seemed unable to resist the French advance and resorted to a series of raids called *chevauchées*. These were not intended to confront or defeat the French armies or even to retake captured towns and cities. Instead, they were an attempt at a scorched-earth policy, destroying mills, farms, and villages and making the countryside as unproductive as possible for the French.

In 1373, the duke of Lancaster, John of Gaunt, launched the Great Chevauchée, a raid intended to cut a swath through French-held territory. This was a costly failure, and the English force finally returned to Bordeaux at Christmas 1373 half-starved and having lost most of its weapons and equipment and many men. The chevauché tactics did not materially slow or even impede the French advance, but they did succeed in making the rural population of Aquitaine hostile to the English cause.

Even worse from an English perspective, their command of the English Channel was threatened. In 1372, while French armies were besieging the port of La Rochelle, a Castilian fleet commanded by Ambrosio Boccanegra attacked a larger English fleet of warships and transports just outside the port. All the English ships were either destroyed or captured, and for the first time since the war began, England lost its control over the English Channel. This was a major blow because it meant that the English ability to freely move men and supplies from England to Aquitaine was curtailed.

In 1375, the two sides came together to negotiate a settlement, but these discussions foundered on the issue of sovereignty over Aquitaine. Edward III insisted that he must have full sovereignty over English possessions in Aquitaine. The French insisted that they should have sovereignty over all French territory and that all Plantagenet territory in France would be subordinate to the House of Valois. Despite the personal intervention of the Pope, no agreement could be reached and the war continued.

A further outbreak of the Black Death in France and England in 1375 slowed the progress of the fighting, and in 1376, the Black Prince died at his home in England. The following year, Edward III died and was succeeded by the ten-year-old son of the Black Prince, Richard II. Due to the youth of the new king, England was effectively ruled during this period by a series of regency councils, with John of Gaunt being one of the most influential members.

Richard was notably less warlike than his grandfather or father, and he sought peace with France and within England. The Peasants' Revolt, which swept England in 1381, was partly a response to high taxes imposed to support the war against France. The revolt was successfully suppressed, but it was clear that the economy of England could not continue to wage war indefinitely.

In 1380, Charles V of France died and was succeeded by his 11-year-old son Charles VI. As in England, the effective rule of France was undertaken by a council comprising the young king's four uncles, the dukes of Burgundy, Berry, Anjou, and Bourbon. Almost as soon as Charles V was dead, the new French king was also faced with a revolt. On his deathbed Charles V, believing that the war with England was almost won, had repealed the unpopular taxes which had been imposed to support the war effort. It quickly became clear that the war was not over, and the council of dukes attempted to re-impose the taxation leading to a large-scale revolt. The dukes were forced to repeal the taxation, leaving them very short of money to continue the war.

While England and France remained technically at war, there was actually relatively little fighting in the period following the ascension of the two new kings. Neither of the new rulers was particularly interested in pursuing the war, and its unpopularity with the mass of people due to high taxes meant that it was only a matter of time before there were moves to formally bring it to an end.

Finally, in the autumn of 1388, the English Parliament sent emissaries to the French court to begin peace negotiations. The problem of Aquitaine was not directly addressed—this was not an attempt to solve the underlying problems which had led to the war. It was a recognition on both sides that the war was bringing them close to complete financial collapse and that it must be ended. Initially, the negotiators agreed not an end to the war but a temporary truce which was planned to last for three years. In fact, the truce would endure for 26 years, but neither England nor France enjoyed a great deal of stability during the peace.

Chapter Five

Second Peace: 1389-1415

"Forget, forgive, conclude and be agreed:
Our doctors say this is no time to bleed."

—King Richard II, Act 1 Scene 1, *Richard II* by William Shakespeare.

In England, the young king Richard brought about a transformation of the English court. War and warfare had been the main focus of his grandfather, Edward III, but instead Richard wanted the royal household to become a more refined place, with an emphasis on art and culture. By the time the truce that ended the second phase of the Hundred Years' War was signed, Richard was 22 years old and, having attained his majority, had taken over the rule of England from the council of regents.

Richard was determined to pursue a policy of peace with France and through this to ensure that the burden of taxation on his people was reduced. This did not sit well with some of his courtiers who were much more enthusiastic about the pursuit of the war. A proposal was put forward in 1393 which would have greatly expanded the extent of English holdings in Aquitaine, but this would also have required the English king to accept the sovereignty of the French king over his French lands. This was unacceptable, and instead, in 1396, an extended truce between France and England was agreed which was intended to last for 28 years. That ensured the war was no longer the main focus in the relationship between England and France, but it did not bring tranquility for Richard.

Although there was some suggestion that King Richard II may have been mentally unstable (something partly attributable to his portrayal in William Shakespeare's play *Richard II*), modern historians think this unlikely, though some accept that the young monarch may have suffered from some form of personality disorder that became more apparent later in his reign. Richard's early reliance on the advice and friendship of a very small group of courtiers angered many influential English nobles, and in 1387, a group of aristocrats who became known as the Lords Appellant took control of Parliament and forced Richard to have many of his closest advisors arrested and executed. By 1389, Richard had regained control, and for eight years, he seemed willing to forget the actions of the Lords Appellant and ruled in harmony with them.

In 1396, in an attempt to draw the royal houses of England and France closer, 29-year-old Richard married the 6-year-old daughter of Charles VI, Isabella of Valois. Then, in 1397, Richard suddenly turned on the surviving members of the former Lords Appellant and had many of them exiled or executed. When Richard's closest ally and advisor John of Gaunt died in 1399, Richard had John's son, Henry of Bolingbroke, who was also the grandson of Edward III and a childhood friend of Richard, disinherited and exiled.

An outraged Henry returned to England with an army, initially claiming that he intended only the take the position of duke of Lancaster, which he claimed was rightfully his. However, it rapidly became clear that Henry had a great deal of support from English nobles, and he was able to declare himself king and to be crowned as Henry IV in October 1399. Richard was arrested and imprisoned, and he died in somewhat mysterious circumstances in February 1400.

Although he enjoyed a great deal of support when he was fighting for the throne, Henry IV spent most of his reign fighting against insurrection and revolt. Major revolts in Wales and Northumberland were countered by English armies, and in several battles, these were commanded by Henry's eldest son, Henry of Monmouth, who proved to be a very effective military leader. The king also suffered from continuing health problems. He had a disfiguring skin condition from which he suffered all his life, but from 1405 onwards he also suffered from recurring bouts of some debilitating disease. Historians cannot agree on precisely this disease was, but in 1413, it finally killed Henry IV, and he was succeeded by his son who became King Henry V.

During the same period, the French monarchy was also suffering from a variety of misfortunes. By 1393, Charles VI had passed through eccentricity into full-blown madness and he was no longer capable of rationally ruling the kingdom of France. Instead his wife, Isabeau of Bavaria, presided over a regency council which included some of the most powerful French nobles. Two men, in particular, the king's uncle Philip the Bold, duke of Burgundy, and his brother Louis I, duke of Orléans, became the main rivals for power. When Philip died in 1404, his son John the Fearless inherited the escalating feud with Louis.

In 1407, Louis was assassinated. The identity of his murder was never finally established, but it was widely believed that John the Fearless had instigated it, something he never denied. Louis's son Charles inherited the title duke of Orléans and appealed to his father-in-law for help. This sparked off the Armagnac-Burgundian Civil War which was fought for the next 30 years, during—but entirely independent from—the Hundred Years' War.

The English did nothing to prevent a civil war which was bound to weaken France. In 1412, the Armagnacs negotiated a treaty with Henry IV in order to prevent the English king supporting the Burgundians. In this treaty, they gave the province of Guyenne to the English king. However, John the Fearless, leader of the Burgundians, also negotiated with Henry in order to assure the supplies of wool which were essential to the Flanders wool trade.

In 1413, John the Fearless fomented a revolt in Paris which led to the city being under the control of the rebels for almost four months during which time there were widespread executions and massacres. The terrified people of Paris appealed to the Armagnacs for help, and during 1414, forces loyal to Charles, duke of Orléans, reclaimed the city. If the English had been content to stay out of France, it seems possible that the growing civil war might have destabilized and permanently weakened the kingdom. Instead, when Henry V took the English throne in 1413, it was clear that he wanted to wage war against France once again. He accepted approaches from the ambassadors of both the Burgundians and the Armagnacs, and in 1414, he began negotiations with the French for his conditions for dropping his claim to the French throne. These included the payment of 1.6 million crowns which was still due as the ransom for John II and English control over Normandy, Touraine, Anjou, Brittany, and Flanders as well as Aquitaine. Henry also demanded that he be allowed to marry Charles VI's youngest daughter, Catherine of Valois.

The French responded with a counter-offer which Henry claimed was a mockery of the English crown. In April 1415, Henry was able to persuade the great council of Parliament to agree to a resumption of the war against France, and in the late summer of 1415, he began to gather troops and a fleet in the ports of southern England. In August 1415, the English king sailed for France with a force of over 10,000 men. His intention was to lay siege to the port city of Harfleur in Normandy and to begin the conquest of French lands in northern France.

Chapter Six

England Triumphant: 1415-1429

"War without fire is like sausages without mustard."

—Jean Juvénal des Ursins, on Henry V's firing of Meaux in 1421.

The English army landed in northwestern France on August 13, 1415 and laid siege to the port city of Harfleur, beginning what became known as the Lancastrian War, the third and final portion of the Hundred Years' War. The siege took longer than expected, and the city did not finally surrender until September 22. Henry's landing in France prompted the warring Burgundians and Armagnacs to declare a truce and to agree to try to defeat the English king before continuing their civil war. With winter approaching, the English army finally began to march on October 8. Henry's intention was to take his army through Normandy to the English-held city of Calais. This was intended as a deliberate provocation, and Henry hoped that this march would draw the French army into battle. He was right, but even he could not have foreseen the scale of the battle that would follow nor its consequences.

On the morning of October 25, 1415, the English and French armies faced one another on a narrow strip of recently plowed land between the forests of Tramecourt and Azincourt, not far from the Somme River. Things didn't look good for the English. They were hungry and weary after marching for more than two weeks, and they were not only massively outnumbered by their French enemies, but they also lacked mounted knights, the best shock-troops of the day.

Historians have disputed the precise numbers of troops involved, but it appears that the English king led a force of somewhere in the region of 1,500 men-at-arms supported by up to 7,000 longbowmen. Facing them was a French army of around 15,000 to 20,000 including large numbers of heavily armed and armored knights on foot and horseback. Even as the two armies faced each other, the French delayed launching an attack while more troops arrived to join their army.

To the French, victory seemed a foregone conclusion, and there was great competition between the French knights for the honor of leading the attack. Around three hours after sunrise, the French launched a massive attack on the English line by mounted knights. They expected that this would smash the English army, but instead it quickly turned into a French disaster. Heavy overnight rain had left the ground between the armies a sea of mud which critically slowed the French charge. The English had driven wooden stakes into the ground the evening before, and these provided an insupportable barrier to the approaching horsemen. Worst of all, the English longbowmen maintained "a terrifying hail of arrow shot" on the approaching cavalry. The French attack slowed, then stopped, then turned into a headlong retreat with wounded and panicked horses plunging through the lines of infantry which were arrayed behind the cavalry.

Next, the French sent in the mass of men-at-arms, thousands of men on foot wearing plate armor. These unfortunates were forced to slog through muddy ground churned up by the attack and retreat of the cavalry while enduring the same constant rain of arrows and picking their way over increasing numbers of their dead and dying comrades. When they finally reached the English lines, the French men-at-arms were exhausted, and they were engaged not just by the English men-at-arms but by the longbowmen who had fired the last of their arrows at point-blank range before taking up swords and cudgels. Unencumbered by armor, these longbowmen were formidable adversaries for troops encumbered by heavy plate and exhausted after slogging through deep mud.

The brutal hand-to-hand fighting lasted for three hours with the English king in the thick of the fighting. By the end, the dead French lay in huge piles in front of the English positions, and thousands had been taken prisoner. By the early afternoon, the English had taken so many prisoners that these numbered several thousand. When the French appeared to be massing for another attack, Henry then took a decision that was to outrage many people at the time—he ordered that most of the French prisoners taken up to that point should be killed as the English could not spare the men to guard them. Many of his knights refused, claiming that such an action was unchivalrous, and the killing was done largely by the longbowmen.

No further French attack came, and it soon became apparent that this slaughter had been unnecessary. The

French withdrew, and the English were left in control of the battlefield that became known as Agincourt. This was a crushing defeat for the French and one of the most decisive and one-sided battles of the whole Hundred Years' War. French casualties were approximately nine times greater than English, and the French army lost a disproportionate number of important commanders during this battle. The dead included three dukes, a viscount, eight counts, an admiral, the master of the crossbowmen, an archbishop, and the mayors of at least nine important French-controlled towns.

The bulk of French casualties at Agincourt were Armagnacs, and the Burgundians lost no time in blaming their enemies for the disastrous defeat. Within ten days of the battle, a Burgundian army marched on Paris and the truce between the two French factions broke down. Henry returned to England and was able to use the victory to gain support for building up his army and planning the next stage of his campaign against France.

Henry returned to France in 1417, and during the next two years, English armies conquered all of Normandy, something they had never before been able to do. A formal treaty was signed between the English and the Burgundians under which Henry would marry Catherine of Valois, daughter of Charles VI. The dauphin was to be disinherited and Henry's heirs would inherit the throne of France.

Despite the signing of the Treaty of Troyes in 1420, large sections of France and in particular the Armagnacs continued to support the dauphin and to oppose the right of an English king to rule France. In 1421, Henry led his armies against the town of Meaux near Paris which was loyal to the dauphin. The siege continued until the town finally surrendered in May 1422. By that time, the English king had become ill, and he went to a castle at Vincennes, near Paris, to recuperate. Instead, Henry V died there on August 31, 1422 aged just 35. Two months later, on October 21, Charles VI of France, by now completely insane, also died. The Hundred Years' War was about to enter its final phase.

Chapter Seven

French Revival: 1429-1453

"Of the love or hatred God has for the English, I know nothing, but I do know that they will all be thrown out of France, except those who die there."

—Joan of Arc

On the death of Henry V, the throne of England passed to his son, Henry VI, who was just nine months old at the time. When Charles VI died, the infant Henry also became king of France according to the stipulations of the Treaty of Troyes. On his deathbed, Henry V passed responsibility for continuing the campaign against France to his brother, John, duke of Bedford. John proved to be an able military commander, and he oversaw notable English victories including the Battle of Verneuil in 1424. Bedford's brother, Humphrey, duke of Gloucester, became lord protector and was responsible for keeping the peace in England.

In France, the string of English victories continued until early 1429 when a young woman from a peasant family came to the attention of the dauphin. This woman, who would later become known as Joan of Arc, claimed to have received visions from God which instructed her to help the dauphin, Charles VII, to throw off the English domination of France. The important and heavily defended city of Orléans was under siege by the English at the time, and

Joan was sent as part of a relief army which arrived at Orléans on April 29, 1429. Just one week later, the siege was ended, the English were defeated, and Joan's presence was considered an important factor. Suddenly, France had a new heroine.

Given fresh hope by their victory at Orléans and by the presence of the divinely inspired Joan, the French army went on the offensive. In what has become known as the Loire Campaign, French troops were able to drive the English and their Burgundian allies from all their positions on the Loire River. On June 18, 1429, the French army, under the command of the duke of Alençon and inspired by the presence of Joan, met the English army in battle near the small village of Patay in north-central France. The English army, under the command of Lord Talbot, did what it had done so successfully before; it deployed large numbers of longbowmen behind a palisade of sharpened wooden stakes. This time, however, the outcome was a complete rout of the English army. English casualties were around 2,000 killed (out of a total of 5,000 men), and many were captured including Lord Talbot. The French lost around 100 men.

Although Joan was not directly involved in the fighting at Patay, this stunning victory was at least partly attributed to her presence on the field. The virtual destruction of the English army at Patay and the loss of men and commanders during the Loire Campaign left central France open to the French, and in the weeks following Patay, they took maximum advantage, retaking land to the north, south, and east of Paris which had previously been held by the English.

Joan was able to persuade the dauphin to march to the city of Rheims where he was crowned King Charles VII of France on July 17, 1429. The French then turned their attention to Paris, then still occupied by the English and their Burgundian allies. In early September, the French army attacked the Saint-Honoré gate into Paris. They failed to enter the city, and Joan was wounded by a crossbow bolt in the thigh. She recuperated over the winter and in the spring of 1430, she was once again ready to undertake military duties. By this time, the young woman had become not just a charismatic symbol of the French struggle for freedom but also a respected and able military commander.

The city of Compiègne, located to the north of Paris, was one of several French cities that had declared allegiance to Charles VII after his coronation. Philip the Good, leader of the Burgundians, decided to besiege the city, and in March 1430, his troops arrived on the Oise River. Joan of Arc, who had apparently decided that she would personally oppose the attack on Compiègne, raised a force of around 400 volunteers and rode to the city. In mid-May of 1430, Joan led her men in an attack on a Burgundian force near the town of Margny, north of Compiègne. She was captured and handed over to the English.

Joan was imprisoned at Rouen, which by that time had become the center of English operations in France. The armies of the kingdom of France launched several attacks towards the city in the hope of rescuing Joan, but all were defeated, and on May 30, 1431, Joan of Arc was burned at the stake. She was 19 years old. Still, the English army never entirely recovered from the defeats suffered in 1429.

In an attempt to counter Charles VII claims to be the legitimate French king, in December 1431, the ten-year-old Henry VI of England was crowned king of France in Notre-Dame Cathedral in Paris. Despite this, large parts of France refused to accept the legitimacy of Henry's claim to the French throne.

The alliance between Burgundy and England was based largely on a personal friendship between John, duke of Bedford, and Philip, duke of Burgundy. Thus, when the duke of Bedford died in 1435, Philip claimed that this released him from his commitment to the English, and in September 1435, the Burgundians signed the Treaty of Arras in which they repudiated their alliance with the English, recognized Charles VII as the rightful king of France, and returned the city of Paris to the control of Charles. Without the support of their Burgundian allies, the English position in France became much less secure.

In the years that followed, the French army made slow but inexorable progress, pushing the English back towards the Channel coast. In 1449, the French captured the strategically vital city of Rouen to the north of Paris. In April 1450, a large English army was attacked and completely defeated at the Battle of Formigny. This was the last important English army in Normandy, and this defeat left all the remaining English strongholds in France vulnerable. Caen fell to the French in July 1450 and Bordeaux and Bayonne in 1451.

Late in 1452, an English force under the command of the venerable John Talbot attacked and recaptured the city of Bordeaux. This left the English with only this city and the port of Calais as their principal possessions in France.

In the spring of 1453, Charles VII prepared his armies for a final assault on the English held lands in France.

The last battle of the Hundred Years' War took place on July 17, 1453, as the English force under the command of John Talbot left Bordeaux and met the French army near the small town of Castillon-sur-Dordogne. The English army was outnumbered, but it attacked the French camp anyway, unaware that the French had established more than 300 guns in a heavily defended artillery park. Artillery and small-arms were still a relatively new addition to the art of warfare in Europe, and no one could foresee how they would change the nature of war and bring to an end the Age of Chivalry.

The advancing English troops were decimated by the French guns, and the battle ended as a rout for the English. John Talbot and his son were both killed during the battle, and the French reclaimed Bordeaux in October leaving the English in control only of the port of Calais. On hearing of the defeat of John Talbot and the recapture of Bordeaux, Henry VI of England appeared to be struck down by total mental incapacity, reportedly failing to respond to anything, including the birth of his son, for more than one year.

Chapter Eight

Peace at Last

"We always have been, we are, and I hope that we always shall be, detested in France."

—Arthur Wellesley, Duke of Wellington

The Battle of Castillon was the last large-scale military action of the series of conflicts which have become known as the Hundred Years' War, but this did not mark the formal end of the war. There was no truce between England and France, but the truth was that both sides were economically exhausted by the war. England in particular was reduced to controlling only a small area of land in France, and this coupled with the mental disintegration of the English king and rising anger in England about the taxes which had been levied to prosecute the war and the loss of trade which was a consequence of the loss of land in France led directly to a series of civil wars which wracked England in the period following the end of the Hundred Years' War.

The inability of Henry VI to rule effectively led to a claim on the throne by Richard, the duke of York. This in turn led to series of conflicts between two rival branches of the House of Plantagenet: the House of York, whose symbol was a white rose, and the House of Lancaster, whose symbol was a red rose. These conflicts, which became known as the Wars of the Roses, continued from 1455 to 1487 and left England in no position to mount a military challenge to the kingdom of France.

There briefly appeared to be a risk of the war reigniting when, in 1474, Charles of Burgundy rose up against the French king, Louis XI. The Burgundians appealed to their old allies the English for support, but King Edward IV of England instead accepted a large cash sum from the king of France and signed the Treaty of Picquigny in 1475 in which the English king formally renounced his claim on the throne of France. Although there had been no major military confrontations between the French and the English for more than 20 years, this treaty marked the formal end of the Hundred Years' War. The Burgundians were defeated, and France continued its progress towards becoming a large, centralized European state.

Even the most fundamental notions about what warfare was and how it was conducted were changed during this conflict. When the Hundred Years' War began, most armies consisted principally of nobles supported by half-trained peasants and of bands of mercenaries who fought for whichever side would pay them the most. In the truces and interludes between periods of war, these companies marauded across the French countryside, looting as they went. As a direct response, the French king had declared the creation of the royal army in 1445—the first-ever standing army created in Europe since the time of the Roman Empire.

After the Battle of Castillon, the roaming bands of mercenaries were given a stark choice—join the new royal army or leave France. Those who refused were ruthlessly hunted down by the new French army which reached a size of almost 6,000 professional soldiers.

The end of the Hundred Years' War also approximately marks the end of the period known as the Age of Chivalry. When the war began, mounted knights equipped with heavy plate armor were the most devastating weapon on the battlefield, equivalent to modern tanks. By the nature of their horses, weapons, and armor, and the amount of time needed to master their use, only the men from the wealthiest families could become knights, and this in turn gave rise to the notion of war as an honorable pursuit which pleased God if it was conducted within certain rules.

The emergence of cannons and personal firearms did not completely eradicate heavy cavalry from the battlefields of Europe, but they certainly changed the nature of warfare. Suddenly, a relatively untrained peasant using a matchlock musket could unseat a charging knight with ease, and cannons could reduce the strongest defense to rubble. The age of mass armies using firearms was a new factor in warfare, and it would directly influence every war which followed.

The peace between France and England did not last long. The Italian Wars, which began in 1494 and lasted until 1559, involved the kingdom of France fighting against the Papal States supported by a number of other European countries including England. During the War of the Spanish Succession (1701-1714), the Seven Years' War (1756-1763), the American War of Independence (1775-1783), and during the French Revolution in 1789, British and French troops fought one another. During the

Napoleonic Wars (1803-1815), there were a series of battles between British and French armies.

It wasn't until 1904 and the signing of the Entente Cordiale that Britain and France finally became allies, and even this alliance failed to completely overcome a legacy of distrust which stretched back to the Hundred Years' War.

Chapter Nine

Legacy

"The French are a logical people, which is one reason the English dislike them so intensely. The other is that they own France, a country which we have always judged to be much too good for them."

—Robert Morley

The Hundred Years' War left a legacy of animosity and distrust between England and France which was never to entirely disappear. The war ended the English dream of a kingdom which combined England with large holdings in mainland Europe. After the war, England retained control only of Calais and the Channel Islands. In 1558, during the Italian Wars, the French finally ejected the English from Calais, leaving them without land in mainland France. The Channel Islands, off the coast of Normandy, remained under English control.

This war also led directly to antipathy in England for anything concerned with France. From the time of the Norman conquest, French had been the main language of diplomacy, the nobility, and even of commerce in England. It was only in 1362, after the conclusion of the first phase of the Hundred Years' War that English officially became the language of England though French was still used in teaching. In 1385, during the second phase of the war, even that use of French was abandoned in England though many French words and words derived from French remained a part of the English language.

Although Edward IV renounced his claim on the French throne in the Treaty of Picquigny in 1475, subsequent English kings and later kings of Great Britain renewed their claim. This claim on the French throne was not finally renounced until 1801. As late as the early 1800s, the English Admiral Nelson would say, "You must hate a Frenchman as you hate the devil."

In France, antipathy to England was just as significant—the phrase *la perfide Albion* ("perfidious Albion") originated in France and alluded to a supposed English liking for treachery and deceit. This view of the English lasted until the twentieth century and beyond. During World War II, when France was occupied by Germany, the leader of Free French Forces (who would later become the president of France), General de Gaulle, was exiled to England. One of his closest advisers later said that "the General must constantly be reminded that our main enemy is Germany. If he would follow his own inclination, it would be England."

Conclusion

The Hundred Years' War was not really a single war at all—it was a series of conflicts between the kingdoms of England and France over a single issue: whether England had the right to own land on the French mainland and a rightful claim on the French throne. The problem began in 1066 when William, duke of Normandy, mounted a successful invasion of England and established himself as king of England while retaining control of his lands in Normandy. Subsequent kings viewed England as only part of their domain with the remainder being located on the other side of the English Channel.

With the consolidation and expansion of the kingdom of France, it was almost inevitable that conflict would arise over the lands in northwestern France claimed by the English. What no one could foresee when war broke out in 1337 was that this conflict would last for over 100 years. Part of the reason for this was that neither side was powerful enough to completely defeat the other. Neither France nor England could afford to support the presence of large armies in the field for long periods, and this war became characterized by a series of bloody conflicts interspersed with long periods of inactivity or truces as both sides struggled to raise enough money to continue the fighting.

The final outcome of the Hundred Years' War was the emergence of a unified France and the loss of all English lands on the European mainland. Its legacy was an enmity that would last for centuries, and in a sense, this war was simply a prelude to many later conflicts between England and France. It was not until the threat posed to Europe by the emergence of Germany at the beginning of the twentieth century that these two countries finally became reluctant allies against the new threat.

Made in the USA
Las Vegas, NV
16 December 2023